i didn't want to grow up

hazyn forsythe

i didn't want to grow up

published by hazyn forsythe in 2025

business enquiries: hazynforsythe@gmail.com

more information:

1. website: https://hazynforsythe.com

2. instagram: @hazynbee and @hazyns

(nb: the links to these sources may be subject to change over time, but are correct at the time of publishing)

copyright © hazyn forsythe (2025)

all rights reserved, including the rights of hazyn forsythe to be identified as the writer, editor, and creative developer of this work, which have been asserted by them in accordance with section 77 of the copyright, designs, and patents act of 1988.

cover design and photography by hazyn forsythe

printed and bound by ingramspark

isbn: 978-1-7396146-1-4

contents

foreword   p.iii
acknowledgements   p.vi
resources   p.vii

think about it   p.1

maybe...   p.3

but...   p.47

vispo trilogy   p.79

foreword
written in july 2025

my first collection held a foreword so long that i can't help but consider it a kind of poem in itself. perhaps, this one will grow into something similar—as with the last, i am allowing myself to freewrite it. there may be imperfections in this foreword, though i would argue that is the result of the one condition we all share: being human.

i take pride in my work; of course i do. when i released 'i think this feeling is hope', it was a culmination of everything i had been through up until that point. it was everything i'd felt and been ready to explore until the age of 21.

i am now 24, three years having passed almost to the month since i published that first collection. some would call it a chapbook, but you'll see later how i feel about that notion—you can call it what you wish, but i will always view it as my 'first collection' in my heart.

several things have changed in my life since that publication was released. i now have my master's qualification in creative writing, from the same university where i did my undergraduate—the university of lincoln, uk.

also, in 2023, i participated in an exhibition planning and artistic contributions team to collaboratively build 'bare' in project space plus on campus. my first major installation poem, 'and she gave me magic', was featured there alongside the wonderful works of peers.

it has also been seven months since the relationship i spoke about throughout much of 'i think this feeling is hope' came to an end. some of these poems explore the process of healing from that, healing which i am learning happens in stages.

several poems in this collection also discuss heavier subjects in less-deniable detail than hints which i weaved into the poems i wrote when i was younger. perhaps that is a symptom of growing up, or perhaps it is just that i have learned more about myself in recent years... and begun to remember more of what i have been through. it was going to get written eventually.

as such, i advise each reader consume this work only at the pace they personally feel comfortable with. that applies to my previous text as well, but i felt the need to say it more plainly here.

i have also included visual and epistolary poems in this collection, which i hadn't been ready to brave doing in 2022—i look forward to learning how these resonate with you alongside the other pieces.

this collection also explores themes i was not ready to address when i put together 'i think this feeling is hope'. the poems in my first collection were all concepts i had come to terms with and had a tidy ending for, though i am now learning that the act of recovery can be messy as fuck. it can scratch, it can bite, and it can scream—all as well as it can weep and laugh.

in my mind, the title of this work speaks for itself in many ways, but i suppose i shall explain: i didn't. i didn't, but i had to.

i had to grow up, in many ways, before i was ready—this collection is just a snippet of that feeling.

and that little child you see in a photoframe on the cover? that was me. i took the cover photo when i was a teenager, in my childhood home. it is a photo containing a photo of when i was much smaller, but no less brave. when i was fighting battles i have since been given names for—names i didn't even have yet when i published 'i think this feeling is hope'.

i am autistic, i have adhd, and i am dyspraxic.

my name is hazyn forsythe,

and i still have growing to do.

acknowledgements

i would like to dedicate this text to three individuals who always heard and nurtured my creative voice. thank you:

eva janoskova

daniele pantano

christopher dows

and, of course, thank you to all others who have listened to, heard, and been there for me in my lifetime.

this may be a tougher read than 'i think this feeling is hope'...

but these things needed to be said.

resources

uk-based resources

mind—mental health support & info

mind.org.uk

samaritans—24/7 crisis support

call 116 123 or visit samaritans.org

youngminds—support for young people & carers

youngminds.org.uk

beat—eating disorder support

beateatingdisorders.org.uk

cruse—bereavement & grief support

cruse.org.uk

nacoa—for children of alcohol-dependent parents

nacoa.org.uk

general & international

trauma-informed resources

traumaresearchfoundation.org

international helplines list

checkpointorg.com/global

the mighty—lived experience communities for chronic illness & mental health

themighty.com

i didn't want to grow up

hazyn forsythe

Who are you?

What did you do to me?

maybe they'll listen
this time

feedback

jamie watched the five-hour
videopoem
then said sorry
for not watching it all in one go.

i forgave him.
i hadn't watched it in one go either.

i hope tuition covers this

i forgot to put it back—
but after what i lost,
i call us even.

new boundaries loading...

why did you hurt me?

why did i believe
it was healthy?

why
did it take
over half a year
to realise
it burned me?

because i trusted
you
i think
so i didn't even blink
when things changed
and the link
between us
began to sink

when you started to drain
my soul out my ears
and replace it with

you
you
you

that hurt

but i believed, because we were
good once, that we must still be

i forgot it is possible for things to
decay
even when they were once good

and that surpassing a bar once
doesn't mean that standard
is met forever

doesn't mean you would always
respect my boundaries

didn't mean...

i almost want to miss you
i almost typed that i did
but my fingers added 'almost'
like i just can't imagine it

i did, i did at first
i missed you and it hurt
but now i miss your bird
his feathers and his chirps

because he knew what 'safe' meant
he knew about boundaries and trust
and he never tried to push me
like you did amidst your...

taxi from hyde park
(thank you, olivia, for saying we could scream)

songs that remind me of you
used to make me feel so damn blue
but tonight i let my rage out
through my chest
and i screamed; i screamed my
fucking best

because you hurt me and i thought it
was love
thought that was what it was
supposed to look like
to be like
to bleed like

and i guess i didn't dream right
'cause i used to dream of you
of us, together, once and forever
but three years was all you could do

but i guess it's a relief
looking back, there was a rift
you'd cut it between us and i'm sure
it hurt you too
but FUCK, why was it always about
YOU?

you really were a vampire
a kind of fucking leech
and i was pulled into your empire
'til you were done with me

sometimes, it's hard to breathe
but i know just what i need
isn't air from your collapsing lungs
but to be loved without having to
bleed

and i cried, i cried and shook
to let it out—that's what it took—
and my sister was my anchor
not you, you fucking...

i'm so scared this could happen to you

i love you with all my heart
and that's why it breaks when i think
of the danger you could be in
if older-you doesn't cover your drink

i love you so fucking much
and that's why i'm terrified
that you'll be hurt by someone's touch
before you can even gather why

the world is dangerous
in ways you don't see
because, sweet sister,
you're only fourteen

but i can't say it to you,
not now, but not never
just... waiting a while
to have this talk together

i won't publish this one
or maybe i will
but i won't show you, yet
it'll be censored, until...

i don't know when

when is a child ready to learn
that there's people out there
who'd wish them hurt?

that there's people who'd
do the worst thing
just for a 'fling'
and consent's beyond what they're
considering

i'm sorry
i'm sorry if this ever happens to you
i'm sorry if i can't stop it
i'm sorry if you ever understand

but i just can't drop it

i saw how you argued last night
about your outfit covering so little
and i understand it's about
autonomy
that clothing isn't permission
but one day you'll realise
that some people just don't listen

to 'no'
to 'don't'
to uncertainty

but for now, i imagine you think
'it can't happen to me'

littlest sister, if i could protect you
from the world, i would
but warn you yet? i don't know
if i should

but I'VE been in danger
i've been fucking endangered
by friends, by lovers, and
total strangers

please, just be careful
but know, as i say
that i'll always be there for
you, always

okay?

this is what i needed

middle
i'm writing this poem for you
i'll redact your name
if you want me to

but i needed to thank you
and you had to know
that i'm so fucking proud
of how much you've grown

you saw me, saw me hurting
and you knew what to do
you knew just how to comfort
because you'd once felt little, too

the tickle-back that soothed you
when we were growing up
the one i'm sure you still crave
when everything feels fucked

as i stood there, tears were pouring
and you paused your world for me
stood next to me at the concert
made sure that i felt seen

i didn't know it would hit me
i had no idea how those songs would hurt
from a retroactive perspective
after new lessons had been learned

but you were there
you were my anchor
and i couldn't help but smile

when he came on stage
and i glanced back
you, little, and her friend had gone wild

tears flooded your eyes
but they were tears of joy, for you

little, i'm proud of you too
i hope, of course, you know that
though you'd probably tell me off
for saying it
in a poem—i'll cut your name if you
want, but...

the true version sits with me
with us, once i've asked our mum
if it's okay to show my sisters
my swear-filled poems when you're
so young

yeah, this is getting soppy
but i can't bring myself to care
because part of being a big sibling
is you always want to be there

i'm sorry for what i've missed
by moving so far away
but i hope, someday, you'll visit
and i can show you where i stay

for more than just a moment
perhaps a couple days
i only have one bed
but the sofa's where i'll stay?

middle, you'll soon learn to drive
that'll be exciting
i extend this invitation here to you
both sisters, here in writing:

come visit me any time
i promise i'll always see you
thank you for being who you are
and loving how you do

gratitude

13th june, 2025. written on co-codamol due to an injured ankle.

dear dan and chris (i'll print two copies so you can keep one each),

yes, i'm writing this in 2025. yes, i graduated in 2022/23. yes, this is in all-lowercase.

because i've spent far too long trying to write the perfect letter and it's made me hold back from finishing this letter at all.

there have been countless—<u>countless</u>—unfinished drafts, attempts at communicating the truth, written across notebooks and google docs and notes on my laptop and <u>who knows</u> where else...

when what was most important was
making sure you knew how
monumental you were to my
development as a creative, a poet, a
writer, and a <u>person</u>. when what
mattered most was the fact that the
support you gave me throughout
university is a significant part of
the reason i remained alive long
enough to graduate—and to return
to do my ma—and to get to the point
i am at now.

in 2022, i published 'i think this feeling is hope' (this font doesn't include italics; please forgive me). technically, most would class it as a chapbook—i consider it my first collection, for the whole book as an object is a poem to me. it was a beginning, a fresh start, a prelude to what i could achieve. it was also one last push at proving to myself i could achieve it.

it is now 2025. 'and she gave me magic', my installation poem made to honour the memory of baget—whom i cared about and miss deeply—was featured in the bare exhibition two years ago.

i am returning to poetry again. at first, it was in bits and pieces. now, i feel like my soul has returned to me.

chris, i want to thank you for how swiftly you noticed and supported me as my personal tutor. for how you built essay structures with me yet simultaneously kept an eye on me during a time when my continued survival was not a guarantee. you were the first to notice my mental health was slipping due to the transition to university, the move from hertfordshire to lincoln, and—at least, had others noticed—the first to step up.

i'll admit, i rebelled against the idea of writing the synopsis first more than once. i wrote the story, pretended i didn't, then wrote a synopsis afterwards and handed you that whilst quietly polishing the story in the background. you probably knew. if you didn't, you do now. i also pretended to write short stories more than once, making up an ending for the hand-in but continuing the piece in secret; i couldn't let go of the characters once i'd lived with them.

dan, you knew me later—though, technically, you met me first (on the offer holder day during which i learned i wished to be taught by you alongside learning how quietly devastating six words could be—'for sale: baby shoes, never worn'). you were no less important, no less fundamental. thank you, too, for everything.

the third-year poetry module, 'poetry & innovative form', taught me who i was and who i wanted to be. it taught me i have the capacity to be that person, to find new ways to work around obstacles and work through feelings until i'd built a dollhouse and recorded videopoems and built soundscapes and poured my heart into more than just pages. i needed to learn that freedom, that expansive range of ways to create that poetry offers beyond the sensible—beyond the logical—and into depths of expression.

both of you may know there were times i did not believe i would make it out the other side of university—times i did not believe my psychosis would heal or my anxiety would be soothed or my depression would take a fucking break—but i did. i graduated first with my ba in creative writing and second with my masters. i sank my soul into both degrees, gave everything i was capable of, and i honestly thought at times that i would drown beneath the weight of everything. yet, you created something invaluable for me—a safe place, a secur

[more will be written]

p.s., may i publish this?

more gratitude

4th july, 2025. no longer on co-codamol, though my ankle is still healing.

i think i was trying to write 'security' or 'secure environment' when i hit my limit for what i could emotionally communicate that day in june. i don't know how almost a month has passed, but... somehow, here we are.

thank you. you have both been a profound influence on my development as an individual and poet (and creative and writer and artist and who-knows-what-else), which i will forever be grateful for.

i almost got upset when i didn't finish this letter in one sitting, especially since i had already written the post-script under the assumption that i would complete my message in only a day. a little hopeful of me, perhaps, but i wouldn't call it foolish.

because i realised in the interim between these two parts that this is something of an epistolary poem—one i would love to include in the collection i am developing, titled 'i didn't want to grow up', which will explore...

well, i suppose you'll just have to see.

i can tell you, though, that your presence throughout university enabled me to nurture parts of myself that hadn't been given enough attention before reaching that environment. it allowed me to safely grow into an artist who became brave enough to use that very word—not only in a whisper, but as an introduction—and a poet who is proud of all aspects of my creative development.

i will remember your support; i intend to get back in touch in the future, beyond these letters, but my email inbox is always open should you wish to reply... if i don't brave delivering this in-person, that is.

i respect you both greatly.

thank you for everything,

                hazyn forsythe

i think we made a discord server once

i'm sorry for all the people they hurt
i don't remember what they said
what happened, what was done...

but i remember how you fell away
after i admitted i didn't remember.

after i panicked and spiralled
because i
hadn't grown past it yet
hadn't learned how to separate
the kid who said those things from
the person i am now

i opened up and i think you thought i
meant it to hurt you
i think you thought i was placing a burden
i think you thought i was telling you to fix it

when i don't even remember those words
falling from my lips

but i do remember being lost
i do remember how afraid i was

and i think i trusted you
i think you helped me, in the way you could
and that meant something
even if i don't remember it

even if, in the end, you had to
set a boundary
a boundary i have since grown to
understand
a boundary that scared me at first

because i hadn't learned that it's
okay to let people leave sometimes

that people stepping away doesn't
mean you don't have value

it just means they needed

                s p a c e

and, whether or not you forgive
the teenager who didn't know better
the teenager who debated how it
felt
the teenager who spilled secrets
like soup

i do

and i'm still grateful for you.

okay

"okay...
okay."
and i'm suspended in midair,
ready for the crash,
the collapse, the fall
from the cliff—
yet it never comes.
he said "okay"?
and it ended—
right then, right there
—for all my struggles
have built up to this.
this moment when i am finally:
acknowledged.
listened to.
understood.
believed.
HEARD.
by the one i thought would never
hear me,
by the one i believed
never could.

growing up, it was
never "okay", it was
but
and
if
then
because
you
need
to
do
what
i
say
...
...

or, perhaps, i need not.
i need not to follow
his word
i need not to follow
his path.
i do not live to copy,
i live to
travel my own journey
to learn, to discover,
to build an identity
where i don't have to
earn my place in
this world
where i never need to
prove my place
my worth
my value
where i never HAVE to showcase my
skills,
but merely
choose to

and, in doing so,
choose to love
who i am
what i do
what i can and cannot do
who i will and will not be
for it is all beautiful, all of it.
and who would think
that a simple "okay"
could be all i've needed?
a subtle "i hear you
and i'm not fighting it,
not saying you're wrong
or challenging your wit",
a simple "okay" that screams
"i'll let you be,
i'll let you live
for now, you're free"

and hopefully
HOPEFULLY
that will be it
and my journey can wander
it can take its twists
and i'll learn and i'll ponder
without feeling amiss
because i'm building
MY world
how I imagined it.

but they won't always hear me

i am not a pincushion

out
of class
i stepped

my time-
out card
was clenched

and then
it bent—
my neck

back
back
back again

my body crumpled
i slumped
i lay on the floor

a dirty floor of secondary school

along the tech and art and
science corridor

alone

i don't know how long it took
for a teacher to find me
i could not move

i could not speak
everything hurt and would not move
they got me into a
wheelchair
they wheeled me to
a room
where i lay
in wait
on white sheets
for help to come
to take me
to...

teachers
paramedics
ambulance

a sharp prick to my finger
a clip on another
a band on my arm to
check my blood-pressure

a rush, a hush, then the next i'd know
bright lights, bed beneath me, hospital ceilings
        one, two, three, light
        one, two, three, light
                one
                two
                three
                light

a laugh
a smile   "are you scared?"

my arms were swinging
i didn't choose that
the bars were up, so i punched metal
over and over
faster and faster
harder and harder

he was preparing a cannula

and he smiled
not in sympathy
but in...

arms held me down
flipped me over
pinned my arm behind my back
muscles clenched and tensed
for i knew that

it would hurt
it would hurt
           IT'S GOING TO HURT

and then they stabbed my hand
anyway

the world went fuzzy and grey

then i was gone

then i woke

a room i'm unsure i was ever in

small, shielded, dim

a memory of visitors who never
came to the hospital with me

but i saw them
they talked to me

then, next i knew, i was in a bed
facing the opposite direction

bright lights, again
strangers, again
but also...

my mum

                                              'MUMMY'

i wanted to say that

'mummy
mummy
mummy

i'm scared

i'm trapped

nothing is right

i can't move

i can't speak

a man laughed at me'

…but i couldn't

no words came out

then, they checked my arms

felt resistance

implied that meant…
pretend

i barely remember what happened next

i was weaned off what my body had deemed toxic

i was recovering, slowly

but

JOLT

JOLT

JOLT

JERK

JERK

JERK

my body still moved on its own

yet never when i told it to

my jaw would jut
my neck would tilt
my shoulders twisted
my arms flung out
my stomach clenched as if punched
my legs... i don't remember

i don't remember having legs

until i sat in a waiting room of
another hospital

where my body still reacted
still twitched
still dystonically ticced
still dropped
still fell
still put me through hell

but i could walk
sometimes
so that meant i was fine

...right?

and then, the 'specialist'

tried to sound 'cool' by swearing
had no idea he was triggering what i
hadn't yet worked through

then, across me, accused me of
faking
but not to me
to my mum
told her it was...

"TEENAGE GIRLS AND THEIR
HORMONES"

then sent me away
maybe home, maybe not, that part
is a blot
there's ink covering that
dark until

i was back in school
trying to adjust
and i dared use my time-out card
just once

and they hunted me down
after five minutes away
because...

that 'specialist' knew how to ruin
more than just one fucking
consultation

he'd told my school:
- not to listen
- not to fuss
- not to 'draw attention'

in words, as such, whether or not
his intention

what little support i had?
it withered away

and my family did not understand
why the tics, they stayed

they believed they should have gone
when the medication left

i didn't understand it either

only now, a decade later, do i know

sometimes neurological damage
does not just 'go'.

the reprise

it's impressive
how callous
how empty, how cold
how cynical you all could be

first, in the south to merely
a child
then—ten years later—to
an adult, to me

which time was worse?
it is hard to tell
the first time, some had
deniability

but—
FUCK
what am i doing?
why am i even considering
forgiving?

i was trapped
i was helpless
i was jolting then motionless
i was silent
then whining
then barely able to speak

i couldn't breathe through the snot
through the tears, through the rot
of this system which once again
failed me

head tilted back
did you care?
no, you snapped

and you mocked
and you blamed
and you did it again

"the thing is,
we KNOW you CAN move"

are you sure about that?
is this where you've sat?
feeling safe, feeling certain no-one
will stop you?

but i will
i'll find a way
i'll make it change

be it a poem or a formal complaint

because—dear a & e—we've got some
fucking beef

if you're determined to paint a liar
of me.

i begged and breathed in snot

it's so heavy
i just want to sleep
why are we doing this again?
what's the point in 'me'?

who are you? who am i?
you're haunting and i'm sick
not possessed but trapped with you

trapped

trapped

trapped

i couldn't move
i choked on snot
i could barely breathe
yet you cared not

i screamed inside
all that came out were whines
then pleas
for my mum, for answers
for some fucking belief

it's pulling me under
it's drowning me

but i finally feel anger
you gave me that
is this the lesson i am to learn?
that i had to suffer again to work
out how to express distaste?

honestly, it was like a race
to see who could dismiss
discount, disappoint me the fastest
to see who could make me hurt for
being honest

you didn't listen
you didn't call her
you didn't even try

and now i'll remember this
for the rest of
my life.

tea parties with fairies

little pieces of pastry
on miniature plates
a few drops of fruit squash
hoping they won't hate
the effort i put in
that it'll be to their taste

because i loved them
i felt them
i felt for them
they were the ones i understood
so i left my tea sets overnight
when we stayed once, near the
woods

i knew how they worked, in some
ways
the everpresent fae
that, perhaps, they might be
watching
if i did just as i'd say

so i always kept to my word
i always held my truth
i always told it carefully
just in case someone should
disbelieve me, doubt me, fail to
understand
or claim i broke a promise, but
my truth would always land

yet some assumed me a liar
some assumed all were
they never saw my ire
but, perhaps, someday
they'll learn

that when your words are chosen
carefully, carefully,
c a r e f u l l y,
it's possible to live only by truth
and not fall to such follies
as to think 'everyone lies'
when, in actuality,

not everybody tries.

shooe

an echo of a memory
not mine, but it should be
perhaps it is, just not...
consciously

of a father, high out his mind
unable to manage a buckle or strap
unable to put a shoe on his...
well, i suppose it was
'his daughter', back then

but what message did it send?
to throw a shoe at a child

learning now, feeling then

i wonder how i processed it
if i processed it at all
that's both the curse and blessing
of having been so small

out

bang
bang
BANG

"...let me in.
let me in, now.
let me in, or i'll..."

shhhhhhhrrrssssst

scrape

push

shove

quickly

sit down, put your back to it

maybe he'll go awa—

BANG

"i said n o w..."

the ground is moving

you're sliding, no matter how much
you press back

the bookshelf, the cabinet,
your own body was not enough

"LET ME IN."

let me out, let me out, let me out

i was trapped inside a box
i still am, sometimes
that box is sometimes flesh-shaped
but sometimes it's more confined
to shape
to standards
to the feeling of walls
to the texture of paint
to h...

why does that place always
come up?
why do we always
go there?
why can't i
stay away from it?
it's just not fucking FAIR

sarah, i agree with you;
        it's not fair,
        it's not fair,
      it's just not fair

yet such a complex worldview
of rules and boundaries and
patterns
was treated as a moral lesson
about what truly mattered

perhaps, it can be true
that you're right
that it's not fair
and still conquer that
cold labyrinth
those
geometrically-questionable stairs

to find
a baby brother
to fulfill
your noble quest
yet when you made your wish
you'd made it from your chest

from your heart
which...

i suppose i should listen to mine
it wanted to say 'hospital'
a wish i then declined

because as much as
                                           miffy
got me through it
with a plushie and a book
and
                            my comfort toys
held tight
on other occasions

    STILL, THEY TOOK AND TOOK

my autonomy
my sense of safety
my understanding of the world

fuck, i think it's hospitals
that make me hurt most to be a 'girl'

sHe'S fAkInG iT fOr AtTeNtIoN

oF cOuRsE sHe Is

and now i'm using meme-formatting
to deter from feeling how much
those words fucking hurt

bEcAuSe It Is FuNnY iF wE wRiTe It
LiKe ThIs

and nobody will realise that
anything's amiss

i titled this poem before writing it

i wanted to explain the feeling

the little voice in my head that
screams 'let me out' over and over

but i ended up on a tangent
because...

and it hurt.

i am only worth your support
    when i perform normality

i am only worth your pride
    when it looks good on paper

i am only worth your compassion
    when it's logical

i am only worth your time
    when it makes sense to you

i am only worth your love
    when i have not disappointed you

i am only worth a bedroom
    when i am a child

i am only worth a house
    when i have a job

i am only worth safety
    when it is on your terms

i am only worth stability
    when i have found it myself

i am not worth it
    without proving myself to you

i am a performance

    you do not know me

        perhaps you never will

vispo trilogy

thanks

i was vulnerable
i was vulnerable
i was vulnerable
i was vulnerable
i was vulnerable
i am vulnerable

fuck you.

waiting for validation

the reply

She said it gave her goosebumps.

www.ingramcontent.com/pod-product-compliance
Lightning Source LLC
Chambersburg PA
CBHW041218070526
44583CB00006B/170